to:

from:

on the occasion of:

MESSIAH

A Photographic Meditation on Handel's Messiah
by Miriam Frost and Keith McCormick

Winston Press

Photography Credits:
Cheryl Walsh Bellville: 1, 7, 25, 29
Gary Bistram: 4-5, 36, 41
Terry Bourcy: 10-11
Joseph A. DiChello, Jr.: ii, 26-27, 38-39
Steve Diehl, North-South Photography: 53
Kay Freeman: 57
Gaytee Stained Glass: Front cover, 13
Geoffrey Gove: 16
Philip MacMillan James, Webb Photos: 35
James LaVigne: 30
Ted McDonough, Webb Photos: 2, 20-21
Tom and Ceil Ramsay, Webb Photos: 55
Cyril A. Reilly: 19, 22, 24, 26, 32-33, 34, 42-43, 44, 45
John F. Scheckler: 6
Ned Skubic: 46, 47, 54
Jerry Stebbins, Webb Photos: 8
Ron Van Zee: 15, 48, 52, 58
John Zombone: 37, 51
Vici Zaremba, North-South Photography: 12, 60

Library of Congress Catalog Card Number: 78-59409
ISBN: 0-03-045721-1
Printed in the United States of America

Winston Press. Inc.
430 Oak Grove
Minneapolis, MN 55403

The text of this book is set in Perpetua Italic
and printed on 80 lb. Productolith Dull by
North Central Publishing Company.

Layout by Ned Skubic.

Comfort ye, comfort ye My people,
saith your God.
Speak ye comfortably to Jerusalem,
and cry unto her, that her warfare is accomplished,
that her iniquity is pardoned.

Isaiah 40:1-2

The voice of him that crieth in the wilderness;
prepare ye the way of the Lord;
make straight in the desert a highway
for our God.

Isaiah 40:3

Ev'ry valley shall be exalted,
and ev'ry mountain and hill made low;
the crooked straight and the rough places plain.

Isaiah 40:4

And the glory of the Lord shall be revealed,
and all flesh shall see it together:
for the mouth of the Lord hath spoken it.

Isaiah 40:5

Thus saith the Lord of Hosts:
Yet once a little while and I will shake
the heavens and the earth,
the sea and the dry land.
And I will shake all nations;
and the desire of all nations shall come.

Haggai 2:6-7

The Lord, whom ye seek,
shall suddenly come to His temple,
even the messenger of the covenant,
whom ye delight in; behold, He shall come,
saith the Lord of Hosts.

Malachi 3:1

But who may abide the day of His coming?
and who shall stand when He appeareth?
For He is like a refiner's fire.

Malachi 3:2

And He shall purify the sons of Levi,
that they may offer unto the Lord an offering
in righteousness.

Malachi 3:3

Behold a virgin shall conceive
and bear a Son,
and shall call His name Emmanuel,
God with us.

Isaiah 7:14

Matthew 1:23

O thou that tellest good tidings to Zion,
get thee up into the high mountain.
O thou that tellest good tidings to Jerusalem,
lift up thy voice with strength;
lift it up, be not afraid;
say unto the cities of Judah, behold your God!

Isaiah 40:9

Arise, shine, for thy light is come,
and the glory of the Lord is risen upon thee.

Isaiah 60:1

For unto us a child is born,
unto us a Son is given,
and the government shall be upon His shoulder;
and His name shall be called Wonderful,
Counsellor,
The Mighty God,
The Everlasting Father,
The Prince of Peace.

There were shepherds abiding in the field,
keeping watch over their flocks by night.

Luke 2:8

And, lo, the angel of the Lord came upon them,
and the glory of the Lord shone
round about them,
and they were sore afraid.

Luke 2:9

And the angel said unto them: Fear not,
for behold, I bring you good tidings of great joy,
which shall be to all people.
For unto you is born this day
in the city of David a Saviour,
which is Christ the Lord.

Luke 2:10-11

*And suddenly there was with the angel
a multitude of the heavenly host
praising God, and saying:*

Luke 2:13

*Glory to God in the highest, and
peace on earth, good will towards men.*

Luke 2:14

21

Rejoice greatly, O daughter of Zion;
shout, O daughter of Jerusalem!
Behold, thy King cometh unto thee;
He is the righteous Saviour,
and He shall speak peace unto the heathen.

Zachariah 9:9-10

Then shall the eyes of the blind be opened,
and the ears of the deaf unstopped.
Then shall the lame man leap as an hart,
and the tongue of the dumb shall sing.

Isaiah 35:5-6

He shall feed His flock like a shepherd;
and He shall gather the lambs with His arm,
and carry them in His bosom,
and gently lead those that are with young.

Isaiah 40:11

Come unto Him, all ye that labour,
ye that are heavy laden, and He will give you rest.
Take His yoke upon you, and learn of Him,
for He is meek and lowly of heart,
and ye shall find rest unto your souls.

Matthew 11:28-29

JESUS ALSO BEING BAPTIZED

Behold the Lamb of God,
that taketh away the sin of the world.

John 1:29

He was despised and rejected of men,
a man of sorrows and acquainted with grief.

Isaiah 53:3

Surely He hath borne our griefs,
and carried our sorrows!
He was wounded for our transgressions,
He was bruised for our iniquities:
the chastisement of our peace was upon Him.

Isaiah 53:4-5

And with His stripes we are healed.

Isaiah 53:5

All we like sheep have gone astray;
we have turned every one to his own way.
And the Lord hath laid on Him
the iniquity of us all.

Isaiah 53:6

Thy rebuke hath broken His heart:
He is full of heaviness.
He looked for some to have pity on Him,
but there was no man,
neither found He any to comfort Him.

Psalm 69:20

Behold, and see if there be any sorrow
like unto His sorrow.

Lamentations 1:12

He was cut off out of the land of the living:
for the transgressions of Thy people
was He stricken.

Isaiah 53:8

But Thou didst not leave His soul in hell;
nor didst Thou suffer Thy Holy One
to see corruption.

Psalm 16:10

Lift up your heads, O ye gates;
and be ye lift up, ye everlasting doors;
and the King of glory shall come in.
Who is the King of glory?
The Lord strong and mighty,
the Lord mighty in battle.
Lift up your heads, O ye gates;
and be ye lift up, ye everlasting doors;
and the King of glory shall come in.
Who is the King of glory?
The Lord of Hosts, He is the King of glory.

Psalm 24:7-10

How beautiful are the feet of them
that preach the gospel of peace,
and bring glad tidings of good things.

Isaiah 52:7
Romans 10:15

Their sound is gone out into all lands,
and their words unto the ends of the world.

Romans 10:18
Psalm 19:4

44

Why do the nations so furiously rage together,
and why do the people imagine a vain thing?
The kings of the earth rise up, and the rulers
take counsel together against the Lord,
and against His Anointed.

Psalm 2:1-2

Let us break their bonds asunder,
and cast away their yokes from us.

Psalm 2:3

Thou shalt break them with a rod of iron;
Thou shalt dash them in pieces
like a potter's vessel.

Psalm 2:9

47

Hallelujah: for the Lord God Omnipotent reigneth.

Revelation 19:6

The kingdom of this world is become the kingdom
of our Lord, and of His Christ; and He shall
reign for ever and ever. King of Kings,
and Lord of Lords.

Revelation 11:15

Hallelujah!

I know that my Redeemer liveth, and that He
shall stand at the latter day upon the earth.
And though worms destroy this body,
yet in my flesh shall I see God.

Job 19:25-26

For now is Christ risen from the dead,
the firstfruits of them that sleep.

I Corinthians 15:20

Since by man came death, by man came also
the resurrection of the dead.
For as in Adam all die, even so in Christ
shall all be made alive.

I Corinthians 15:21-22

The trumpet shall sound, and the
dead shall be raised incorruptible,
and we shall be changed.
For this corruptible must put on incorruption
and this mortal must put on immortality.

I Corinthians 15:52-53

Then shall be brought to pass
the saying that is written:
Death is swallowed up in victory!

I Corinthians 15:54

Worthy is the Lamb that was slain,
and hath redeemed us to God by His blood,
to receive power, and riches, and wisdom,
and strength, and honour, and glory, and blessing.
Blessing and honour, glory and power,
be unto Him that sitteth upon the throne,
and unto the Lamb, for ever and ever.

Revelation 5:9, 12-13

Amen.